POP HITS for the
INSTRUMENTAL SOLOIST

Play-Along Tracks with Full Performance Recordings!

BREAKAWAY

Words and Music by
MATTHEW GERRARD, BRIDGET BENENATE
and AVRIL LAVIGNE

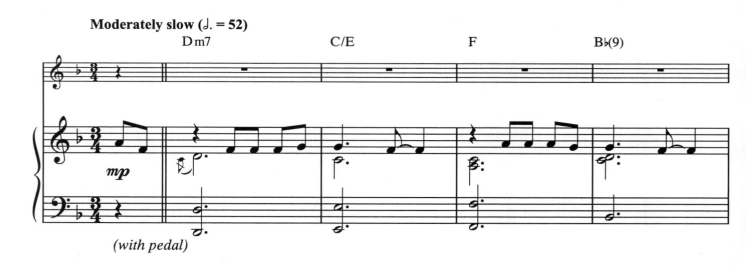

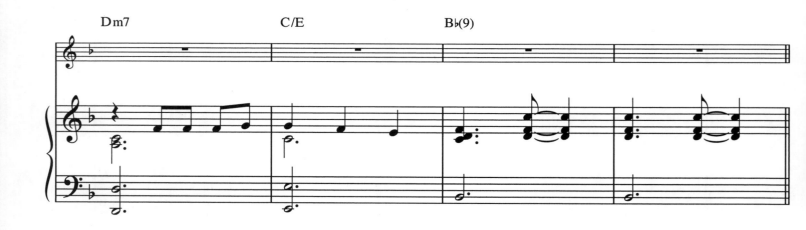

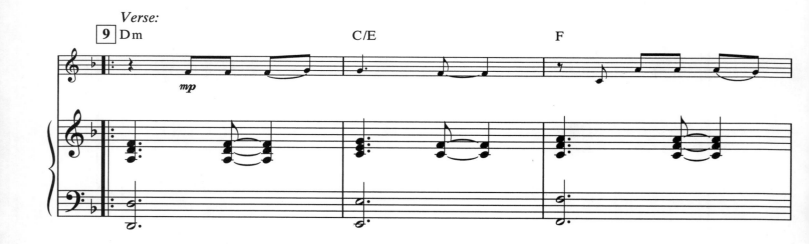

3

4

6

WHEN YOU TELL ME THAT YOU LOVE ME

Words and Music by
ALBERT HAMMOND and JOHN BETTIS

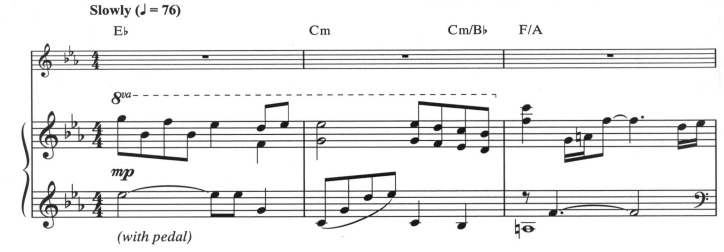

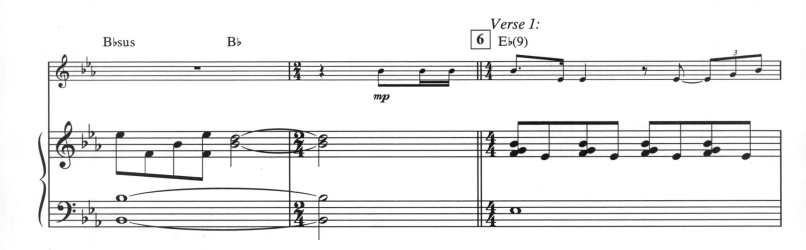

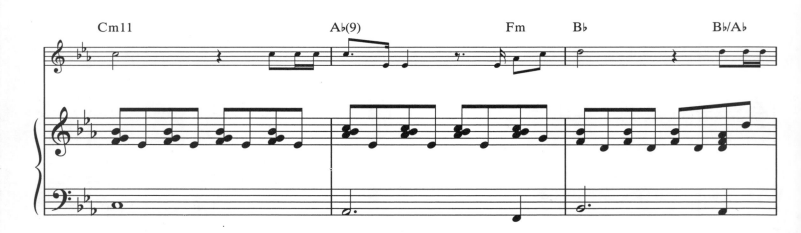

When You Tell Me That You Love Me - 4 - 1
IFM0515CD

When You Tell Me That You Love Me - 4 - 2
IFM0515CD

EVERYTHING BURNS

Words and Music by
BEN MOODY

14

(with pedal)

Verse 2:

35

THE NOTEBOOK
(Main Title)

Written by
AARON ZIGMAN

Slowly, with expression (♩ = 69)

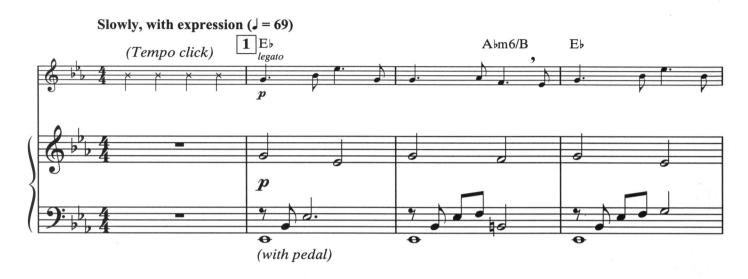

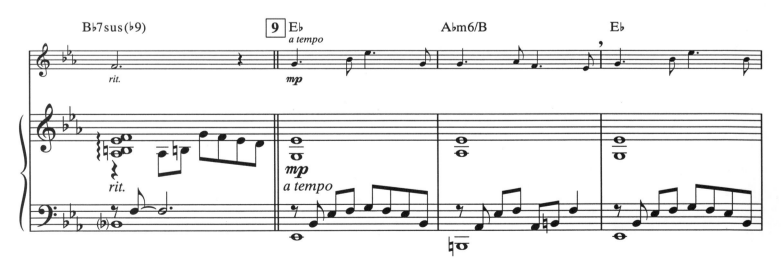

The Notebook - 3 - 1
IFM0515CD

The Notebook - 3 - 3
IFM0515CD

YOU RAISE ME UP

Words and Music by
ROLF LOVLAND and
BRENDAN GRAHAM

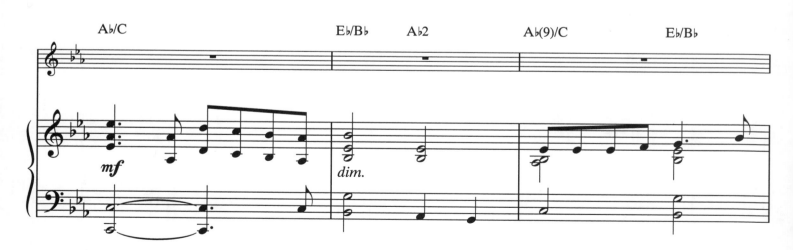

You Raise Me Up - 4 - 1
IFM0515CD

22

You Raise Me Up - 4 - 4
IFM0515CD

THE PRAYER

Italian Lyric by
ALBERTO TESTA and TONY RENIS

Words and Music by
CAROLE BAYER SAGER and DAVID FOSTER

Slowly, with expression (♩ = 72)

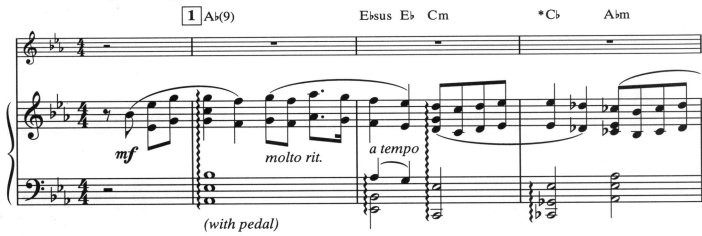

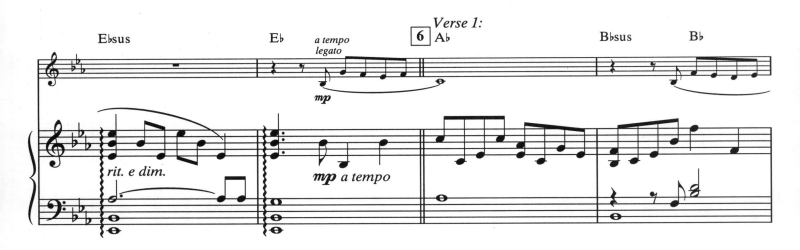

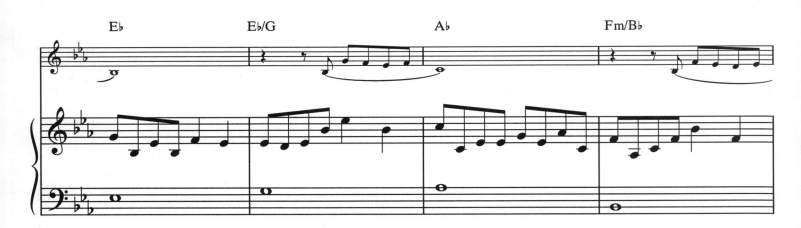

*C♭ = B♮

The Prayer - 5 - 1
IFM0515CD

The Prayer - 5 - 2
IFM0515CD

The Prayer - 5 - 4
IFM0515CD

Chorus:

57

* Fb = E♮

UNTITLED
(How Can This Happen to Me?)

Words and Music by
SIMPLE PLAN

Moderately slow (♩ = 92)

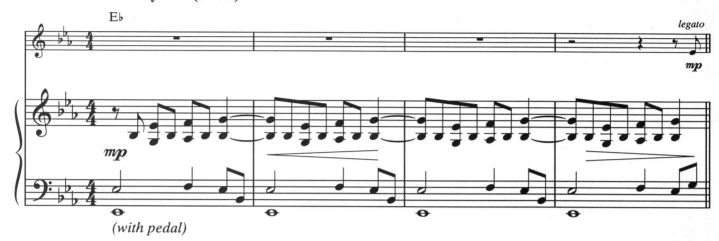

Untitled - 5 - 1
IFM0515CD

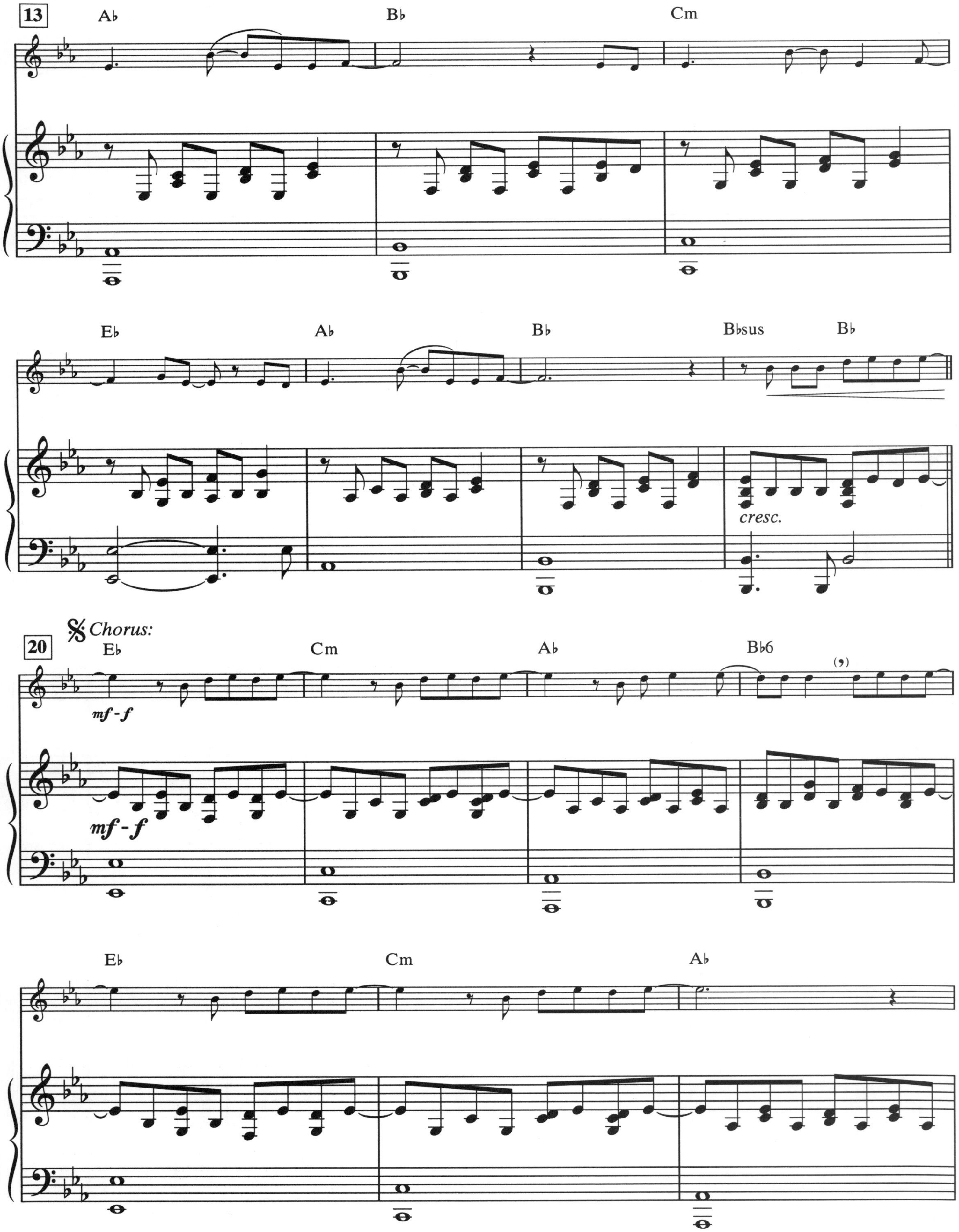
13
A♭
B♭
Cm
E♭
A♭
B♭
B♭sus
B♭
cresc.
Chorus:
20
E♭
Cm
A♭
B♭6
mf - f
mf - f
E♭
Cm
A♭

INSIDE YOUR HEAVEN

Words and Music by
ANDREAS CARLSSON, PER NYLEN
and SAVAN KOTECHA

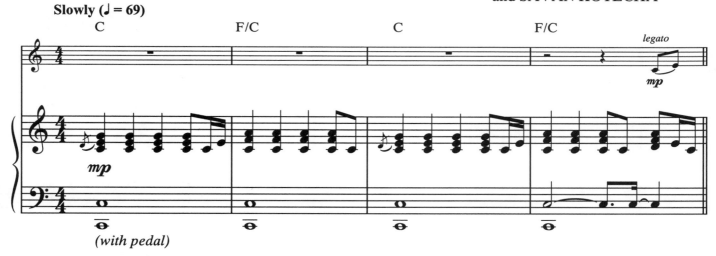

Inside Your Heaven - 4 - 1
IFM0515CD

36

TO WHERE YOU ARE

Words and Music by
RICHARD MARX and
LINDA THOMPSON

Slowly, with expression (♩ = 69)

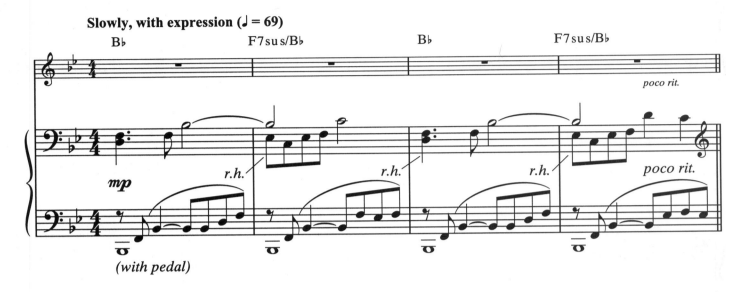

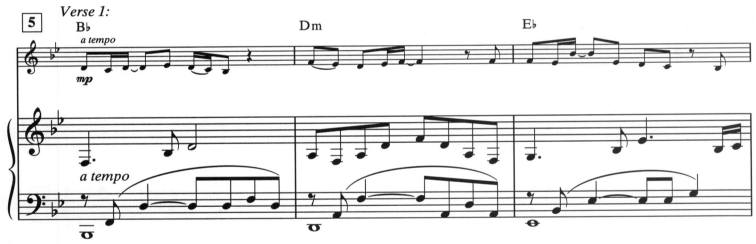

To Where You Are - 4 - 1
IFM0515CD

To Where You Are - 4 - 4

WHEN YOU SAY YOU LOVE ME

Music by MARK HAMMOND
Lyrics by ROBIN SCOFFIELD

When You Say You Love Me - 4 - 1
IFM0515CD

When You Say You Love Me - 4 - 2
IFM0515CD

44

When You Say You Love Me - 4 - 3
IFM0515CD

BRIDGE OVER TROUBLED WATER

Words and Music by
PAUL SIMON

48

Bridge Over Troubled Water - 3 - 3
IFM0515CD